BEI GRIN MACHT SICH IHR WISSEN BEZAHLT

- Wir veröffentlichen Ihre Hausarbeit,
  Bachelor- und Masterarbeit

- Ihr eigenes eBook und Buch -
  weltweit in allen wichtigen Shops

- Verdienen Sie an jedem Verkauf

Jetzt bei www.GRIN.com hochladen
und kostenlos publizieren

Bibliografische Information der Deutschen Nationalbibliothek:

Die Deutsche Bibliothek verzeichnet diese Publikation in der Deutschen National-
bibliografie; detaillierte bibliografische Daten sind im Internet über http://dnb.d-
nb.de/ abrufbar.

Impressum:

Copyright © 2011 GRIN Verlag
Druck und Bindung: Books on Demand GmbH, Norderstedt Germany
ISBN: 9783668785762

Dieses Buch bei GRIN:

https://www.grin.com/document/438387

Ismail Baniadam

Computer assisted Language Learning

GRIN Verlag

Inhalt

Abstract

The use of technology in language learning and teaching programs is very essential. The present study was set out to investigate the effects of E-mail writing on improving EFL learners' written communication and autonomy. The participants of the study were 44 female and male sophomore students, by the age of 18-21 who were randomly assigned to the two groups of experimental and control. Each group consisted of 22 participants. The course lasted for 5 months, and was held in one of the universities in Urmia, Iran. The first group (experimental group) sent their assignments through emails in addition to the traditional class activities but the second group (control group) had the traditional class and assignments were handed in hard copies. For measuring the written communication, a pre-test and post-test was administered to both groups. The pre- and post-tests were criterion reference tests (recognition tests and productive writing activities), based on the materials covered in the class. The pre- and post-tests were parallel recognition tests and productive writing tasks. In order to measure the participants' level of autonomy, the Learner Autonomy Questionnaire, developed by Kashefian (2002), with 40 items in a five-point Likert scale was given to them. The obtained data was analyzed through the SPSS software. The results of this study will be useful for language teachers, learners, administrators and material developers.

Keywords: Computer assisted language learning (CALL); electronic mail (E-mail); written communication; learner autonomy

1. Introduction

Until quite recently, "computer-assisted language learning (CALL) was a topic of relevance mostly to those with a special interest in that area. Recently, though, computers have become so widespread in schools and homes and their uses have expanded so dramatically that the majority of language teachers must now begin to think about the implications of computers for language learning" (p. 1) [1]. As cited by Toyoda (2001), Learner autonomy has been widely discussed in L2 research [2], [3], [4]."Increasingly, the use of modern technology, such as email, the Internet, HTML editors, is coupled with cooperative approaches to and the positive effects of technology on language learning in general has been demonstrated" (p. 1) [2]. A careful analysis of the literature illustrates how little is known about how technology affects the exercise of learner autonomy. It is envisaged that the success of autonomous learning would be greatly influenced by learners' computer literacy and their beliefs in technology-incorporated learning [2].

2. Background

Language existed long before writing, emerging maybe simultaneously with sagacity, abstract thought and genus of human beings. With the advent of computers into academic classrooms, many changes happened in writing process. For example, Costanzol (1994), for the effectiveness of writing via computer commented that "computers serve as enactive models. They offer physical analogies to the mental and perceptual activities of writing and give inexperienced writers access to alternatives that might otherwise remain invisible" (p. 17) [5]. Since 1960s, CALL programs in USA were designed to evaluate the efficacy of CAI (Computer Assisted Instruction) on the basis of experimental issues with relation to traditional instructional modes [6]. In these days, exercises included grammar and syntax drills, translation and dictation. But it has grown from research projects to the effectiveness of application of CALL to class instructional programs [7]. In the 1970s, with the introduction of language laboratories which were influenced by Audio Lingual Method (ALM), a new room to CALL work stations was opened [8]. Before using of CALL, the term CALI (Computer Assisted Language Instruction) was used, which gets its origin from

CAI (Computer Assisted Instruction) [8]. Warshauer (1996), defined CALL as acronym for Computer Assisted Language learning and it is related to the use of computer for language teaching and learning [1]. Warschauer (1996) and Warschauer & Healey (1998), identified three historical phases of CALL, classified as their pedagogical and methodological approaches [1], [9]:

1. Structural CALL: Conceived in the 1950s and implemented in the 1970s and 1980s.
2. Communicative CALL: Become prominent in the 1980s to 1990s.
3. Integrative CALL: Embracing Multimedia and the Internet from 2000 onwards.

Table.1. Warschauer's three stages of CALL

Stage	1970s–1980s: Structural CALL	1980s–1990s: Communicative CALL	21st Century: Integrative CALL
Technology	Mainframe	PCs	Multimedia and Internet
English-teaching paradigm	Grammar translation and audio-lingual	Communicative language teaching	Content-Based, ESP/EAP
View of language	Structural (a formal structural system)	Cognitive (a mentally constructed system	Socio-cognitive (developed in social interaction)
Principal use of Computers	Drill and practice	Communicative exercises	Authentic discourse
Principal objective	Accuracy	And fluency	And agency

CMC (Computer Mediated Communication) has existed in primitive form since the 1960s. It is the single computer application to date with the greatest impact on language teaching and it has only become wide-spread in the last 20 years [1]. E-mail is one of the ways of sending a message or written essay or letter from one computer to another via Internet. Today, use of e-mail is very common in language learning. It is about 4 decades that computers are used in language learning. So that, this is one of the most important of human invention, in which learners can communicate with speakers and other learners of the target language during 24 hours in a day without any limitation, from anywhere that they want such as school, home work and etc. There are two types of communication via internet:

1. Synchronous or real time communication, in which people can have a simultaneous conversation by typing at their keyboard by using special programs such as Moos And Chat rooms. It allows for interaction between teacher and student outside the class situation, or between small or large groups as an interactional discussion.

2. Asynchronous (not simultaneous) communication, in which by using tools such as electronic mail (E-mail), which allows everyone to make their own messages and convey their own feelings and desires at their time and pace. They can also use the web to find authentic materials such as newspapers, articles, and magazines and search millions of fields around the world.

On the other hand, learner autonomy has been a buzz word in foreign language education in the past decades which has modified traditional learning drills and by developing self-access language centers around the world, language teaching is now seen as language learning and it has placed the learner at the centre of language learning education [4]. There is a tremendous attention to learner autonomy, self-directed learning, self-access systems, individualized or independent learning in language learning during the last 2 decades. The Council of Europe (COE) established a Modern Language Project in 1971 and one of the results of this project was the establishment of the Centre de Researches et d' Applications en Languages (CRAPEL) at University of Nancy, France. CRAPEL project was based on providing adults with opportunities for life-long learning. The founder of it was Yves Chalan, whom by many is considered to be the father of autonomy in language learning.

But as he died in 1972, he could not document his field and Henry Holec, became the leader of CRAPEL. So that, Holec's project reported to COE is considered as a key early document on autonomy in language learning. As a consequence, the term "learner autonomy" was first defined by Henri Holec in 1981 and after that time, he was known as the father of learner autonomy. Holec (1981), defined learner autonomy as "the ability to take charge of one's own learning which is not inborn but must be acquired either by natural means or formal learning, i.e. in a systematic, deliberate way and also to take charge of one's learning is to have the responsibility for all the decisions concerning all aspects of this learning" (p. 1) [4]. "Students, who trust in their technological tools, are able to make full use of the tools to support their autonomous learning" (p. 3) [2].

In Iran, because native language is Farsi and English is as a foreign language and also because of the lack of access to native speakers in educational settings, CALL can help learners to compensate this lack and help them to practice English by watching films, listening to music or pronunciation of native speakers and learning individually. Especially, learning through CALL is useful for those who are shy or feel threatened in class or who are introverts and do not have opportunity to show themselves in academic situations. Although, a number of attempts have been made to learn about academic writing tasks across the college curriculum, relatively few studies have focused on computer-based writing activities and reaching autonomy [2]. Accordingly, there are researches which have investigated Iranian students' foreign language learning attitudes, attitude towards CALL and relationship between these variables [10]. But in Iran there is a gap in area like learning writing through CALL in universities or in institutes and schools and also the effect of technology on learners' autonomy. So the purpose of this study is to investigate the effect of E-mail on the improvement of EFL learners' written communication and autonomy which attempts to address that gap.

3. Methodology

3.1. Participants

This study was conducted with the students at Urmia University. In both experimental and control groups there were 22 female and male students, by the age of 18-21, who were sophomore students. The time of the class of group 1 was from 8:30 a.m. until 10:30 a.m. and for group 2 the time was from 11 a.m. to 1 p.m. on the same day. Duration of the course was 5 months in Urmia University, Iran. Students in each group were native speakers of Turkish, Kurdish and Persian.

3.2. Materials

In order to determine the role of e-mail on the development of written communication and autonomy of students, a test of language proficiency (Oxford Placement Test) was administered among 55 young sophomore learners out of whom those whose scores lie between one SD below and above the mean were selected for the study. Two EFL groups were chosen randomly. The participants of the study were included forty-four sophomore learners in Urmia University. In order to determine their level of proficiency, Oxford Placement Test was used. Each test consisted of two sub-tests and contained 100 questions of grammatical structures, which administered in the form of multiple-choice items. The Marking Kit with Users' Guide and Diagnostic Key contained a separate marking overlay for each page of the test, which was scored objectively. Subtotals for each student added up, to give total scores and the tests were placed in rank order. For measuring the written communication, a pre-test and post-test was used and for measuring learners' autonomy, a questionnaire was given to students. The T-test was used in both groups. Both groups took pre-test. After the pre-test, learners were received the instruction based on the materials covered in the class. The first group (experimental group) had the chance to work with e-mails and send their assignments through e-mails in addition to the traditional class activities but the second group (control group) did not have this opportunity and just had the traditional class. The learners were involved in a parallel test and productive writing task at the end of the treatment (used as post-test). A Criterion Reference Test based on the materials covered in the class was administered to the participants (a recognition test and a productive writing activity). After pre-test, both groups were involved in post-tests (a parallel recognition test and a productive writing activity). A pilot study was conducted to check the reliability and validity of the instruments before the study. Then performance of the two groups in the pre-test and post- test was investigated to determine the efficacy of instruction. In order to determine the correlation between the pre-tests and post-tests, the Pearson-Product Moment Formula was used. In this study an autonomy questionnaire was given to them in order to measure their level of autonomy which was developed by Kashefian (2002) [11]. It consists of two main parts. The first part refers to the demographic information of the participants and the second part includes 40 items in a five-point Likert scale, all of which about the role of autonomy in L2 learning. It was used in a study to investigate the interrelationship of autonomy, motivation and academic performance of Persian L2 learners in distance education contexts by Hashemian & Heidari in 2011 [12]. Questions are about learners' perceptions of role of teacher, role of learner, self-evaluation, goal of learner, planning, learners' ability, progression, mistakes and errors which learners commit and time of learning which can be followed in FL classrooms that can help in development of learner autonomy was given to them. A pilot study was conducted to check the reliability and validity of the instrument before the study. As to internal reliability of the questioner, Cronbach Alpha which was used which was 0.80 and for the validity of questionnaire, it was looked into by some professors of Shahrekord and Shiraz Universities and confirmed to be valid [12]. Students' responses were converted into numerical scale. Then, the obtained data were analyzed through the SPSS software and the statistical results of T-test and descriptive statistics reported.

3.3. Data Analysis

At the very beginning of the first session of the research, the researcher revealed to the participants the purpose of instruction during which they received the treatment. They were made aware that participation in the research was totally voluntary and any observed evaluation either in the pre- and post-test or during the whole process of the research would solely be used for the purpose of the research. In order to answer the research questions, the t-test analysis was employed. A t-test is used for comparing the means of two samples (or treatments), even if they have different numbers of replicates. In simple terms, the t-test compares the actual difference between two means in relation to the variation in the data (expressed as the standard deviation of the difference between the means). The two sample t-test simply tests whether or not two independent populations have different mean values on some measure. But Before carrying out any t-test analysis, it was necessary to check the sample for outliers or extreme scores. For this purpose, the boxplot was checked for the proficiency test scores of both groups (technology and traditional). A boxplot is a way of summarizing a set of data measured on an interval scale. It is often used in exploratory data analysis. It is a type of graph which is used to show the shape of the distribution, its central value, and variability. The picture produced consists of the most extreme values in the data set (maximum and minimum values), the lower and upper qualities, and the median [13].

3.4. Procedure

Two EFL groups of sophomore learners were chosen randomly. Both classes were held with the learners of Urmia University. In both experimental and control groups there were 22 female and male students, by the age of 18-21, who were sophomore students. The time of the class of group 1 was from 8:30 a.m. until 10:30 a.m. and for group 2 the time was from 11 a.m. to 1 p.m. on the same day. The reason for conducting the research with sophomore learners was because they were studying English as a foreign language, so that they were more easily accessed to computer and write via it asynchronously. At the very beginning of the first session of the research, the researcher revealed to the participants the purpose of instruction during which they received the treatment. They were made aware that participation in the research was totally voluntary and any observed evaluation either in the pre- and post-test or during the whole process of the research would solely be used for the purpose of the research. After that, the researcher asked those voluntarily to give their e-mail addresses to participate in the research and send their home works via internet. On the same session (one), the professor introduced the course book for them to prepare for the next time. On sessions two and three, the professor taught the new lesson of Letter Writing which was an introduction to Letter Format and the writing process and gave a short description about business letters, heading, address titles and abbreviations, salutation, body, complementary close, signature, punctuation styles, the form of a letter, and all the elements which should be regarded in writing a letter was introduced to learners. The aim of this activity was to prepare learners for the main task which was supposed to be implemented during the following sessions. Then, participants were asked to talk about their ideas about letters and write a letter for the next session and those who were supposed to work via computer send their letters via e-mail to the researcher and the others write on the paper and bring it to the class for correction. In the third session after students give their writings to their professor, some of them read their letters to the class and the professor wanted the peers to check each other's mistake if there was. Some of the letters were such as:

My dear friends;

I came back to Earth and now I live on Earth and I feel great here because I am with my family, my old friends, my school, teachers and…but the most important reason for feeling awesome is that here is not rainy always. We have all four seasons. In spring I feel ardor of blossoms. The blossoms which shine beneath the Sun's rays. I eat all kind of fruits at summer. The fruits which are ripe because of the Sun. It is great to feel the heat of the Sun in autumn and you could not imagine how enjoyable is making a snowman on cold but sunny days of winter.

I wish you could one day feel them but for this you have to wait another seven years.

Love

Margot

Dear Mr. Donnelly,

Maybe writing these sentences causes to grow the flames of hatred toward me. I was very young about five or six when I shoplifted for the first time. At first it did not made me feel good but then..., everything became usual. I can claim that I enjoyed it; even I did not need what I stole. Years passed, I grew and the sense of shoplifting became more and more strong.

During all these years, I have not met someone to stop me. My sister who I learnt shoplifting from, my mother who ignored it, my friend who followed me without any objection. I do not want to justify myself and I know it was I who was the main guilty of all these events and also the main victim.

Now, everything is going to change, for, I want to. Since the day we have met I always think about your speech and I agree that you are right. Why I should not throw away those unimportant things that waste my energy? I have the talent to be a good, intelligent, useful person for myself. So, why I do not try?

Thank you for your help. I hope I merit all the nice words you used to protect me, by compensating.

Truly,

Wicky

It provides the readers with detailed information on the layout of business letters as well as different punctuation styles and letter formats. On session four after guidance and correcting lexical and grammatical errors, learners were provided with the new words perceived to be problematic for them by the instructor who spent some time practicing them to make sure that their meanings were clear to them. Then some more on Introductory and Closing Parts was introduced continues with explanation of other introductory and concluding parts. It also addressed the envelope. On session five, Letters on business situations were introduced and the participants were asked to compare their own writings with their partners' and share them with the class. During each lesson, the students listen carefully to get a general idea of the text, and they note down key words and phrases (i.e. the content words which they think are important in later text reconstruction). The tutor described how the task was going to be implemented and how they should approach it. The explanation in each part was followed with practical examples and sample sentences. Letters on Social Situations were introduced during sessions six and seven. In order to set the ground the teacher showed a couple of illustrations from their books and some explanations or questions were accompanied with each one. The procedures were like those of the previous sessions. The goal here was to do with recommendation letters, cover letters and writing resumes. In order to avoid the difference of input between the two groups negatively affects the result of the research, the utmost attempt was made to make the provided input for both groups as much similar as possible. The rationale behind this attempt was the fact that the researcher wished to make sure that the results of the research was mainly attributed to the effect of technology on writing, rather than effect of traditional methods on it. Accordingly, all the procedures were the same in both groups. For session eight, they were asked to write recommendation letters and write a resume with some exercises followed the book. For the next session, learners were required to write their daily activities they were reminded to make use of the instructed structure and a couple of learners read out their schedules and did a number of exercises mostly taken from The Letter Writing book. Session nine and ten related to the Writing Business Email letters which covered email uses, formatting business emails, email logistics and courtesies in using email. On session eleven, the questioners were given to learners to check their level of autonomy during these eleven sessions and know how much learners reach to the level of autonomy. Then they had review from the entire thing which they learned and wrote to get ready for their final exam and also for their post-test examination which was on session twelve (the last session). In each session, lots of samples were included to help learners further internalize the material. Sometimes the sample letters did not completely match the explanations provided. The goal of exercises and web tasks were to test the learners' understanding of contents and practice their competence.

4. Results

The results of the Cronbach's Alpha test of internal consistency showed that the reliability of the autonomy questionnaire was 0.80 which is considered a good amount of reliability. Therefore, this questionnaire was utilized for estimating the amount of learner autonomy among the learners. As can be observed in the following figure, there were neither outliers nor extreme values in the sample. Therefore, the t-test could be carried out for analyzing the data.

Figure 1. Boxplot for the proficiency scores

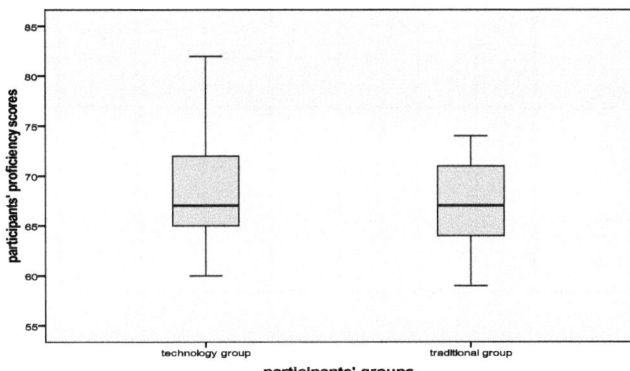

According to Table 4.1, the results of the independent samples t-test showed that there was not a significant difference between the two groups in their pretest scores: t $(33.52) = -1.54$; p > 0.05. This result is logical and acceptable because the treatment started after the pretest; therefore, the lack of difference at the beginning was reasonable.

Table 4.1. Independent samples t-test for the pre-test

		Levene's Test for Equality of Variances		t-test for Equality of Means				
		F	Sig.	t	df	Sig. (2-tailed)	Mean Diffe rence	Std. Error Differe nce
pretest scores	Equal variances assumed	6.58	.014	-1.55	39	.13	-.51	.33
	Equal variances not assumed			-1.54	33.52	.13	-.51	.33

The results of the independent samples t-test (table 4.2), showed that there was not a significant difference between the technology and traditional groups with respect to the posttest scores. The result of the analysis can be summarized: t (40) = 0.53; p > 0.05. Consequently, the null hypothesis of no difference between the two participant groups was accepted.

Table 4.2. Independent samples t-test for the post-test

		Levene's Test for Equality of Variances		t-test for Equality of Means				
		F	Sig.	t	df	Sig. (2-tailed)	Mean Difference	Std. Error Difference
postt est score s	Equal variances assumed	.001	.98	.53	40	.60	.17	.31
	Equal variances not assumed			.53	39. 98	.60	.17	.31

As Table 4.3, indicates, the mean scores of the participants were very close to each other (9.62 for the technology group and 9.45 for the traditional group). This means that there was no significant difference between the two groups in the post-test.

Table 4.3. Descriptive statistics for the post-test

	participants' groups	N	Mean	Std. Deviation	Std. Error Mean
posttest scores	technology group	21	9.62	1.02	.22
	traditional group	21	9.45	1.00	.22

On table 4.4, the t-test analysis also showed that there was not a significant difference between the technology and traditional groups with regard to the degree of autonomy. Both participant groups were very close to each other with regard to the amount of autonomy which was based on the autonomy questionnaire: $t(40) = 0.08$; $p > 0.05$. Therefore, the null hypothesis of no difference between the two groups with respect to autonomy was accepted.

Table 4.4. Independent samples t-test for the autonomy

		Levene's Test for Equality of Variances		t-test for Equality of Means				
		F	Sig.	t	df	Sig. (2-tailed)	Mean Difference	Std. Error Difference
autonomy	Equal variances assumed	.09	.77	.08	40	.94	.29	3.56
	Equal variances not assumed			.08	38.70	.94	.29	3.56

Checking the mean scores of the two groups (table.4.5) shows that the two scores were very close to each other (95.48 for the technology group and 95.19 for the traditional group.

Table 4.5. Descriptive statistics for the autonomy

	participants' groups	N	Mean	Std. Deviation	Std. Error Mean
autonomy	technology group	21	95.48	10.42	2.28
	traditional group	21	95.19	12.55	2.74

In order to investigate the effect of treatment in the groups, a matched t-test was used. As the Table 4.6, illustrates, the results of the paired samples t-test revealed that there was a significant difference between the performances of the participants in the pretest and posttest. The following table shows the results for the two participant groups.

$t(19) = -6.33; p < 0.05$

$t(20) = -6.15; p < 0.05$

These significant differences could be the consequence of one term of working with the participants in both groups during the treatment.

Table 4.6. Paired samples t-test for the technology group

		Paired Differences					Sig.
		Mean	Std. Deviation	Std. Error Mean	t	df	(2-tailed)
Pair 1	Pretest scores-posttest scores	-2.30	1.63	.36	-6.33	19	.00

Table 4.7. Paired samples t-test for the traditional group

		Paired Differences					Sig.
		Mean	Std. Deviation	Std. Error Mean	t	df	(2-tailed)
Pair 1	pretest scores - posttest scores	-1.46	1.09	.24	-6.15	20	.00

5. Discussion & Conclusion

The main goals of this study were to find the effects of technology on learners' autonomy and writing ability. It was supposed that, the use of these variables would help learners in achieving a self-directed learning in everyday life. The study showed that there was not a significant difference between those who worked with technology from those who did not work with technology and took part in traditional classes.

It also indicated that technology did not have any effect on writing and autonomy of the learners. The results of this study are to some extent similar to those obtained by Reinders (2006, 2007), who found that using asynchronous system did not encourage learners to develop their autonomy [14], [15]. In that study, the author needed more training to clarify program for student. However there are some studies that show the opposite of these findings. For example, Toyoda (2001) claimed that "the technology can have a positive impact on learner autonomy when learners have extensive experience with technology" (p. 1) [2]. He furthered that "it also can have a positive impact on autonomy only when learners perceive technology as a useful tool" (p. 11) [2]. The positive effects of technology on language learning also have been demonstrated by Warschauer (1996) [1]. The common things among all these studies is that, by connecting classroom learning which is formal, with other learning outside the class situation, which is informal, students may see University learning experience as an extension to the future [16]. We will achieve to this goal the time that learners take responsibility for their own learning by the help of the teacher from the beginning levels of education.

Different justifications can be brought for this finding. First of all, the participants of this study were advanced university students and may be in lower levels there may be some differences but in advanced levels it is hard. Advanced university students have the experience of working with computers for some years and their writing ability has improved to some extent because of dealing with the language before. It seems that for them, the use of technology or the lack of it does not influence their writing ability or autonomy. Most of the time university professors are doubtful about the use of technology in their classes, and do not know whether it is influencing students' ability or not. According to this study, the use of emails in letter writing classes does neither influence the participants' letter writing ability nor their autonomy. Further, there are some restricted factors in formal learning which interfere to the development of learner autonomy due to administrative and institutional issues. As Yumuk (2002), describes "the majority of learners undergo the process of learning through recitation in which the teacher is the authority rather than facilitator" (p. 143) [17]. The other point is that most of learners want to become autonomous but as they used to rely on the teacher from the beginning of the school, they see it as a difficult task. So that it is teachers' duty to show learners how to become autonomous in language learning. And finally, developing learner autonomy is difficult in an environment such as Iran where many changes should be done from traditional methods to new ones in teaching and because of these changes, both learners and teachers have problem in changing their ways of teaching to become autonomous.

6. References

1. M. Warschauer, Computer Assisted Language Learning: an Introduction, In Fotos S. (ed.) Multimedia language teaching, Tokyo: Logos International, 3-20, (1996).

2. E. Toyoda, Exercise of Learner Autonomy in Project-Oriented CALL, CALL-EJ Online ISSN 1442-438X, Vol. 2, No. 2, January 2001,etsuko@unimelb.edu.au, (2001).

3. L. Dam, Learner autonomy in practice, In I. Gathercole (Ed.) Autonomy in language learning. London: Bourne Press, 16-37, (1990).

4. H. Holec, Autonomy and Foreign Language Learning. Oxford: Pergamon (1981).

5. W. Costanzol, Reading, Writing, and thinking in an age of electronic literacy, In Cynthia L. Selfe & Susan Hilligoss (Eds). Literacy and computers: The complications of teaching and learning with technology (pp. 11-21). New York: Modern Language Association, (1994).

6. C. Atkinson and A. Wilson, (eds.), Applications of CAL in CAL, A Book of Readings, Chapter 3. New York: Academic Press, (1969).

7. K. Evelyn and P. Olivier William, Computer-assisted language learning Investigation On Some Design and Investigation Issues, Department of Measurement, Evaluation, and Computer Applications, The Ontario Institute for Studies in Education, 252 Bloor Street West, Toronto, Ontario, M5.S I V6, (1987).

8. N. Gündüz, Computer Assisted Language Learning, Journal of Language and Linguistic Studies, Vol.1, No.2, October 2005, nazgunduz@yahoo.com, (2005).

9. M. Warschauer & D. Healey, Computers and language learning: an overview. Language Teaching 31: 57-71, (1998).

10. M. Rahimi & S. Yadollahi, Success in learning English as a foreign language, Journal of Procedia Computer Science 3: 167–174, (2011).

11. S. Kashefian, An investigation into college EFL learners' beliefs demonstrating their predispositions Towards learner autonomy, Unpublished master's thesis, Shiraz University, Shiraz (2002).

12. M. Hashemian, & K. Heidari Soureshjani, The Interrelationship of Autonomy, Motivation, and Academic Performance of Persian L2 Learners in Distance Education Contexts, Theory and Practice in Language Studies, Vol. 1, No. 4, pp. 319-326, (2011).

13. V. Easton, & McColl's, J. Journal of Statistics Glossary v1.1, (2010).

14. H. Reinders, Supporting self-directed learning through an electronic learning environment, In T. Lamb & H. Reinders (Eds.), Supporting independent learning: issues and interventions (219-238). Frankfurt am Main: Peter Lang Publishing (2006).

15. H. Reinders, Big brother is helping you: Supporting self-access language learning with a student monitoring system. System, 35(1), 93-111(2007).

16. D. Allford, & N. Pachler, Language, autonomy and the new learning environments (1st ed.). Frankfurt am Main: Peter Lang Publishing, (2007).

17. A. ŞLetting Yumuk, Go of control to the learners: The role of the Internet in promoting a more autonomous view of learning in an Academic translation course, Educational Research, 44(2).141-156, (2002).

7. Appendix

LEARNER AUTONOMY QUESTIONNAIRE

Name: Age: Sex:

Directions: Please show how much you agree or disagree with the following statements by circling the numbers which match your answers.

Strongly Agree	Agree	Neutral	Disagree	Strongly Disagree
1	2	3	4	5

I believe . . .

1	The teacher should offer help to me.	1	2	3	4	5
2	The teacher should tell me what my difficulties are.	1	2	3	4	5
3	The teacher should tell me how long I should spend on an activity.	1	2	3	4	5
4	The role of the teacher is to tell me what to do.	1	2	3	4	5
5	The teacher should always explain why we do an activity in class.	1	2	3	4	5
6	The role of the teacher is to help me learn effectively.	1	2	3	4	5
7	The teacher knows best how well I am.	1	2	3	4	5
8	The role of the teacher is to create opportunities for me to practice.	1	2	3	4	5
9	The role of the teacher is to set my learning goals.	1	2	3	4	5
10	The teacher should be an expert at showing learners how to learn.	1	2	3	4	5
11	The teacher should give me regular tests.	1	2	3	4	5
12	I need the teacher to tell me how I am progressing.	1	2	3	4	5

13	It is important to me to see the progress I make.	1	2	3	4	5
14	I know how to check my works for mistakes.	1	2	3	4	5
15	Having my works evaluated by others is helpful.	1	2	3	4	5
16	Having my works evaluated by others is scary.	1	2	3	4	5
17	I have a clear idea of what I need of English.	1	2	3	4	5
18	I like trying out new things by myself.	1	2	3	4	5
19	My language learning success depends on what I do in classroom.	1	2	3	4	5
20	My own efforts play an important role in successful language learning.	1	2	3	4	5
21	I myself can find the best way to learn the language.	1	2	3	4	5
22	I know how to plan my learning.	1	2	3	4	5
23	I know how to ask for help when I need.	1	2	3	4	5
24	I know how to set my learning goals.	1	2	3	4	5
25	I know how my language learning progresses.	1	2	3	4	5
26	I know how to study languages well.	1	2	3	4	5
27	I know how to study other subjects well.	1	2	3	4	5
28	I have the ability to learn a language successfully.	1	2	3	4	5
29	I have the ability to write accurately in English.	1	2	3	4	5
30	I have the ability to get the score I try for on my next English test.	1	2	3	4	5
31	I know how to find an effective way to learn English.	1	2	3	4	5
32	I know best how well I learn.	1	2	3	4	5
33	I have been successful in language learning.	1	2	3	4	5

34	I have my own ways of testing how much I have learned.	1	2	3	4	5
35	I am average at language learning.	1	2	3	4	5
36	Making mistakes is a natural part of language learning.	1	2	3	4	5
37	Making mistakes is harmful in language learning.	1	2	3	4	5
38	It is possible to learn a language in a short time.	1	2	3	4	5
39	Learning a language takes a long time.	1	2	3	4	5
40	I am above average at learning.	1	2	3	4	5